SO-ASI-506

'WHAT IF SHE ISN'T
HAPPY – DOES
SHE THINK MEN
ARE HAPPY IN
THIS WORLD?
DOESN'T SHE
KNOW HOW
LUCKY SHE IS?'

BETTY FRIEDAN
Born 1921, Peoria, Illinois, USA
Died 2006, Washington, DC, USA

Selection taken from *The Feminine Mystique*, first published
in 1963.

FRIEDAN IN PENGUIN MODERN CLASSICS
The Feminine Mystique

BETTY FRIEDAN

*The Problem that Has
No Name*

PENGUIN BOOKS

PENGUIN CLASSICS

UK | USA | Canada | Ireland | Australia
India | New Zealand | South Africa

Penguin Books is part of the Penguin Random House group
of companies whose addresses can be found at
global.penguinrandomhouse.com.

This selection first published 2018
001

Copyright © Betty Friedan, 1963

The moral rights of the author have been asserted

All rights reserved

Set in 10.25 / 12.75 pt Dante MT Std
Typeset by Jouve (UK), Milton Keynes
Printed in Great Britain by Clays Ltd, St Ives plc

ISBN: 978-0-241-33926-8

www.greenpenguin.co.uk

Penguin Random House is committed to a
sustainable future for our business, our readers
and our planet. This book is made from Forest
Stewardship Council® certified paper.

Contents

The Problem that Has No Name   1

The Passionate Journey   25

The Problem that Has No Name

The problem lay buried, unspoken, for many years in the minds of American women. It was a strange stirring, a sense of dissatisfaction, a yearning that women suffered in the middle of the twentieth century in the United States. Each suburban wife struggled with it alone. As she made the beds, shopped for groceries, matched slip-cover material, ate peanut butter sandwiches with her children, chauffeured Cub Scouts and Brownies, lay beside her husband at night, she was afraid to ask even of herself the silent question: 'Is this all?'

For over fifteen years there was no word of this yearning in the millions of words written about women, for women, in all the columns, books and articles by experts telling women their role was to seek fulfilment as wives and mothers. Over and over women heard in voices of tradition and of Freudian sophistication that they could desire no greater destiny than to glory in their own femininity. Experts told them how to catch a man and keep him, how to breastfeed children and handle their toilet training, how to cope with sibling rivalry and adolescent rebellion; how to buy a dishwasher, bake bread, cook gourmet snails, and build a swimming pool with their own hands; how to dress, look, and act more feminine and make marriage more exciting; how to keep their husbands from dying young and their sons from growing into delinquents. They were taught to pity the neurotic, unfeminine, unhappy women who wanted to be poets or physicists or presidents. They learned that truly feminine women do not want careers, higher education, political rights – the independence and the opportunities that the old-fashioned feminists fought for. Some women, in their forties and fifties, still remembered painfully giving up those dreams, but most of the younger women no longer even thought about them. A thousand expert voices applauded their femininity, their adjustment, their new maturity. All they had to do was devote their lives from earliest girlhood to finding a husband and bearing children.

By the end of the 1950s, the average marriage age of women in America dropped to twenty, and was still dropping, into the teens. Fourteen million girls were engaged by seventeen. The proportion of women attending college in comparison with men dropped from 47 per cent in 1920 to 35 per cent in 1958. A century earlier, women had fought for higher education; now girls went to college to get a husband. By the mid fifties, 60 per cent dropped out of college to marry, or because they were afraid too much education would be a marriage bar. Colleges built dormitories for 'married students', but the students were almost always the husbands. A new degree was instituted for the wives – 'PhT' (Putting Husband Through).

Then American girls began getting married in high school. And the women's magazines, deploring the unhappy statistics about these young marriages, urged that courses on marriage, and marriage counsellors, be installed in the high schools. Girls started going steady at twelve and thirteen, in junior high. Manufacturers put out brassières with false bosoms of foam rubber for little girls of ten. And an advertisement for a child's dress, sizes 3–6x, in the *New York Times* in the fall of 1960, said: 'She Too Can Join the Man-Trap Set.'

By the end of the fifties, the United States birthrate was overtaking India's. Statisticians were especially astounded at the fantastic increase in the number of babies among college women. Where once they had two children, now they had four, five, six. Women who had once wanted careers were now making careers out of having babies. So rejoiced *Life* magazine in a 1956 paean to the movement of American women back to the home.

In a New York hospital, a woman had a nervous breakdown when she found she could not breastfeed her baby. In other hospitals, women dying of cancer refused a drug which research had proved might save their lives: its side effects were said to be unfeminine. 'If I have only one life, let me live it as a blonde', a larger-than-life-sized picture of a pretty, vacuous woman proclaimed from newspaper, magazine, and drugstore ads. And across America, three out of every ten women dyed their hair blonde. They ate a chalk called Metrecal, instead of food, to shrink to the size of the thin young models. Department-store buyers reported that American women, since 1939, had become three and four sizes smaller. 'Women are out to fit the clothes, instead of vice versa,' one buyer said.

Interior decorators were designing kitchens with mosaic murals and original paintings, for kitchens were once again the centre of women's lives. Home sewing became a million-dollar industry. Many women no longer left their homes, except to shop, chauffeur their children, or attend a social engagement with their husbands. Girls were growing up in America without ever having jobs outside the home. In the late fifties, a sociological phenomenon was suddenly remarked: a third of American women now worked, but most were no longer young and very few were pursuing careers. They were married women who held part-time jobs, selling or secretarial, to put their husbands through school, their sons through college, or to help pay the mortgage. Or they were widows supporting families. Fewer and fewer women were entering professional work. The shortages in the nursing, social work, and teaching professions caused crises in almost every American city. Concerned over the Soviet Union's lead in the space race, scientists noted that America's greatest source of unused brainpower was women. But girls would not study physics: it was 'unfeminine'. A girl refused a science fellowship at Johns Hopkins to take a job in a real-estate office. All she wanted, she said, was what every other American girl wanted – to get married, have four children, and live in a nice house in a nice suburb.

The suburban housewife – she was the dream image of the young American women and the envy, it was said, of women all over the world. The American housewife – freed by science and labour-saving appliances from the drudgery, the dangers

4

of childbirth, and the illnesses of her grandmother. She was healthy, beautiful, educated, concerned only about her husband, her children, her home. She had found true feminine fulfilment. As a housewife and mother, she was respected as a full and equal partner to man in his world. She was free to choose automobiles, clothes, appliances, supermarkets; she had everything that women ever dreamed of.

In the fifteen years after the Second World War, this mystique of feminine fulfilment became the cherished and self-perpetuating core of contemporary American culture. Millions of women lived their lives in the image of those pretty pictures of the American suburban housewife, kissing their husbands good-bye in front of the picture window, depositing their station wagonsful of children at school, and smiling as they ran the new electric waxer over the spotless kitchen floor. They baked their own bread, sewed their own and their children's clothes, kept their new washing machines and dryers running all day. They changed the sheets on the beds twice a week instead of once, took the rug-hooking class in adult education, and pitied their poor frustrated mothers, who had dreamed of having a career. They gloried in their role as women, and wrote proudly on the census blank: 'Occupation: housewife'.

For over fifteen years, the words written for women, and the words women used when they talked to each other, while their husbands sat on the other side of the room and talked shop or politics or septic tanks, were about problems with their children, or how to keep their husbands happy, or improve their children's school, or cook chicken, or make slip-covers. Nobody argued whether women were inferior or superior to men; they were simply different. Words like 'emancipation' and 'career' sounded strange and embarrassing; no one had used them for years. When a Frenchwoman named Simone de Beauvoir wrote a book called *The Second Sex*, an American critic commented that she obviously 'didn't know what life was all about', and besides, she was talking about French women. The 'woman problem' in America no longer existed.

If a woman had a problem in the 1950s and 1960s, she knew that something must be wrong with her marriage, or with herself. Other women were satisfied with their lives, she thought. What kind of a woman was she if she did not feel this mysterious fulfilment waxing the kitchen floor? She was so ashamed to admit her dissatisfaction that she never knew how many other women shared it. If she tried to tell her husband, he didn't understand what she was talking about. She did not really understand it herself. For over fifteen years women in America found it harder to talk about this problem than about sex. 'I don't know what's wrong with women today,' a suburban psychiatrist said uneasily. 'I only know something is wrong because most of my patients happen to be women. And their problem isn't sexual.' Most women with this problem did not go to see a psychoanalyst, however. 'There's nothing wrong really,' they kept telling themselves. 'There isn't any problem.'

But on an April morning in 1959, I heard a mother of four,

having coffee with four other mothers in a suburban development fifteen miles from New York, say in a tone of quiet desperation, 'the problem'. And the others knew, without words, that she was not talking about a problem with her husband, or her children, or her home. Suddenly they realized they all shared the same problem, the problem that has no name. They began, hesitantly, to talk about it. Later, after they had picked up their children at nursery school and taken them home to nap, two of the women cried, in sheer relief, just to know they were not alone.

Gradually I came to realize that the problem that has no name was shared by countless women in America. As a magazine writer I often interviewed women about problems with their children, or their marriages, or their houses, or their communities. But after a while I began to recognize the telltale signs of this other problem. I saw the same signs in suburban ranch houses and split-levels on Long Island and in New Jersey and Westchester County; in colonial houses in a small Massachusetts town; on patios in Memphis; in suburban and city apartments; in living-rooms in the Midwest. Sometimes I sensed the problem, not as a reporter, but as a suburban housewife, for during this time I was also bringing up my own three children in Rockland County, New York. The groping words I heard from other women, on quiet afternoons when children were at school or on quiet evenings when husbands worked late, I think I understood first as a woman long before I understood their larger social and psychological implications.

Just what was this problem that has no name? What were the words women used when they tried to express it? Sometimes a woman would say, 'I feel empty somehow . . . incomplete.' Or she would say, 'I feel as if I don't exist.' Sometimes she blotted out the feeling with a tranquillizer. Sometimes she thought the problem was with her husband, or her children, or that what she really needed was to redecorate her house, or move to a better neighbourhood, or have an affair, or another baby. Sometimes, she went to a doctor with symptoms she could hardly describe: 'A tired feeling . . . I get so angry with the children it scares me . . . I feel like crying without any reason.' (A Cleveland doctor called it 'the housewife's syndrome'.) A number of women told me about great bleeding blisters that break out on their hands and arms. 'I call it the housewife's blight,' said a family doctor in Pennsylvania. 'I see it so often lately in these young women with four, five, and six children, who bury themselves in their dishpans. But it isn't caused by detergent and it isn't cured by cortisone.'

Sometimes a woman would tell me that the feeling gets so strong she runs out of the house and walks through the streets. Or she stays inside her house and cries. Or her children tell her a joke, and she doesn't laugh because she doesn't hear it. I talked to women who had spent years on the analyst's couch, working out their 'adjustment to the feminine role', their blocks to 'fulfilment as a wife and mother'. But the desperate tone in these women's voices, and the look in their eyes, was the same as the tone and the look of other women, who were sure they had no problem, even though they did have a strange feeling of desperation.

A mother of four who left college at nineteen to get married told me:

> I've tried everything women are supposed to do – hobbies, gardening, pickling, canning, being very social with my neighbours, joining committees, running PTA [Parent-Teacher Association] teas. I can do it all, and I like it, but it doesn't leave you anything to think about – any feeling of who you are. I never had any career ambitions. All I wanted was to get married and have four children. I love the kids and Bob and my home. There's no problem you can even put a name to. But I'm desperate. I begin to feel I have no personality. I'm a server of food and a putter-on of pants and a bedmaker, somebody who can be called on when you want something. But who am I?

A twenty-three-year-old mother in blue jeans said:

> I ask myself why I'm so dissatisfied. I've got my health, fine children, a lovely new home, enough money. My husband has a real future as an electronics engineer. He doesn't have any of these feelings. He says maybe I need a vacation, let's go to New York for a weekend. But that isn't it. I always had this idea we should do everything together. I can't sit down and

read a book alone. If the children are napping and I have one hour to myself I just walk through the house waiting for them to wake up. I don't make a move until I know where the rest of the crowd is going. It's as if ever since you were a little girl, there's always been somebody or something that will take care of your life: your parents, or college, or falling in love, or having a child, or moving to a new house. Then you wake up one morning and there's nothing to look forward to.

A young wife in a Long Island development said:

I seem to sleep so much. I don't know why I should be so tired. This house isn't nearly so hard to clean as the cold-water flat we had when I was working. The children are at school all day. It's not the work. I just don't feel alive.

In 1960, the problem that has no name burst like a boil through the image of the happy American housewife. In the television commercials the pretty housewives still beamed over their foaming dishpans and *Time*'s cover story on 'The Suburban Wife, an American Phenomenon' protested: 'Having too good a time . . . to believe that they should be unhappy.' But the actual unhappiness of the American housewife was suddenly being reported – from the *New York Times* and *Newsweek* to *Good Housekeeping* and CBS Television ('The Trapped Housewife'), although almost everybody who talked about it found some superficial reason to dismiss it. Some said it was the old problem – education: more and more women had education, which naturally made them unhappy in their role as housewives. 'The road from Freud to Frigidaire, from Sophocles to Spock, has turned out to be a bumpy one,' reported the *New York Times* (28 June 1960).

> Many young women – certainly not all – whose edu-
> cation plunged them into a world of ideas feel stifled
> in their homes. They find their routine lives out of
> joint with their training. Like shut-ins, they feel left
> out. In the last year, the problem of the educated
> housewife has provided the meat of dozens of
> speeches made by troubled presidents of women's
> colleges who maintain, in the face of complaints,
> that sixteen years of academic training is realistic
> preparation for wifehood and motherhood.

There was much sympathy for the educated housewife. ('Like a two-headed schizophrenic . . . once she wrote a paper on the Graveyard poets; now she writes notes to the milkman. Once she determined the boiling point of sulphuric acid; now she determines her boiling point with the overdue repairman . . . The housewife often is reduced to screams and tears . . . No one, it seems, is appreciative, least of all herself, of the kind of person she becomes in the process of turning from poetess into shrew.')

Home economists suggested more realistic preparation for housewives, such as high-school workshops in home appliances. College educators suggested more discussion groups on home management and the family, to prepare women for the adjustment to domestic life. No month went by without a new book by a psychiatrist or sexologist offering technical advice on finding greater fulfilment through sex.

A male humorist joked in *Harper's Bazaar* (July 1960) that the problem could be solved by taking away woman's right to vote. ('In the pre-19th Amendment era, the American woman was placid, sheltered and sure of her role in American society. She left all the political decisions to her husband and he, in turn, left all the family decisions to her. Today a woman has to make both the family *and* the political decisions, and it's too much for her.')

A number of educators suggested seriously that women no longer be admitted to the four-year colleges and universities: in the growing college crisis, the education which girls could not use as housewives was more urgently needed than ever by boys to do the work of the atomic age.

The problem was also dismissed with drastic solutions no one could take seriously. (A woman writer proposed in *Harper's* that women be drafted for compulsory service as nurses' aides and babysitters.) And it was smoothed over with the age-old panaceas: 'love is their answer', 'the only answer is inner help', 'the secret of completeness – children', 'a private means of intellectual fulfilment', 'to cure this toothache of the spirit – the simple formula of handing one's self and one's will over to God'.[1]

The problem was dismissed by telling the housewife she

doesn't realize how lucky she is – her own boss, no time clock, no junior executive gunning for her job. What if she isn't happy – does she think men are happy in this world? Does she really, secretly, still want to be a man? Doesn't she know yet how lucky she is to be a woman?

The problem was also, and finally, dismissed by shrugging that there are no solutions: this is what being a woman means, and what is wrong with American women that they can't accept their role gracefully? *As Newsweek* put it (7 March 1960):

She is dissatisfied with a lot that women of other lands can only dream of. Her discontent is deep, pervasive, and impervious to the superficial remedies which are offered at every hand . . . An army of professional explorers have already charted the major sources of trouble . . . From the beginning of time, the female cycle has defined and confined woman's role. As Freud was credited with saying: 'Anatomy is destiny.' Though no group of women has ever pushed these natural restrictions as far as the American wife, it seems that she still cannot accept them with good grace . . . A young mother with a beautiful family, charm, talent and brains is apt to dismiss her role apologetically. 'What do I do?' you hear her say. 'Why nothing. I'm just a housewife.' A good education, it seems, has given this paragon among women an understanding of the value of everything except her own worth . . .

And so she must accept the fact that 'American women's unhappiness is merely the most recently won of women's rights', and adjust and say with the happy housewife found by *Newsweek*:

> We ought to salute the wonderful freedom we all have and be proud of our lives today. I have had college and I've worked, but being a housewife is the most rewarding and satisfying role . . . My mother was never included in my father's business affairs . . . she couldn't get out of the house and away from us children. But I am an equal to my husband; I can go along with him on business trips and to social business affairs.

The alternative offered was a choice that few women would contemplate. In the sympathetic words of the *New York Times*:

> All admit to being deeply frustrated at times by the lack of privacy, the physical burden, the routine of family life, the confinement of it. However, none would give up her home and family if she had the choice to make again.

Redbook commented:

> Few women would want to thumb their noses at husbands, children and community and go off on their own. Those who do may be talented individuals, but they rarely are successful women.

The year American women's discontent boiled over, it was also reported (*Look*) that the more than 21,000,000 American women who are single, widowed, or divorced do not cease even after fifty their frenzied, desperate search for a man. And the search begins early – for seventy per cent of all American women now marry before they are twenty-four. A pretty twenty-five-year-old secretary took thirty-five different jobs in six months in the futile hope of finding a husband. Women were moving from one political club to another, taking evening courses in accounting or sailing, learning to play golf or ski, joining a number of churches in succession, going to bars alone, in their ceaseless search for a man.

Of the growing thousands of women currently getting private psychiatric help in the United States, the married ones were reported dissatisfied with their marriages, the unmarried ones suffering from anxiety and, finally, depression. Strangely, a number of psychiatrists stated that, in their experience, unmarried women patients were happier than married ones. So the door of all those pretty suburban houses opened a crack to permit a glimpse of uncounted thousands of American housewives who suffered alone from a problem that suddenly everyone was talking about, and beginning to take for granted, as one of those unreal problems in American life that can never be solved – like the hydrogen bomb. By 1962 the plight of the trapped American housewife had become a national parlour game. Whole issues of magazines, newspaper columns, books learned and frivolous, educational conferences, and television panels were devoted to the problem.

Even so, most men, and some women, still did not know that this problem was real. A bitter laugh was beginning to be heard from American women. They got all kinds of advice from the growing armies of marriage and child-guidance counsellors, psychotherapists, and armchair psychologists, on how to adjust to their role as housewives. No other road to fulfilment was offered to them in the middle of the twentieth century. Most adjusted to their role and suffered or ignored the problem that has no name. It can be less painful, for a woman, not to hear the strange, dissatisfied voice stirring within her.

It is no longer possible to ignore that voice, to dismiss the desperation of so many American women. This is not what being a woman means, no matter what the experts say. For human suffering there is a reason; perhaps the reason has not been found because the right questions have not been asked, or pressed far enough. I do not accept the answer that there is no problem because American women have luxuries that women in other times and lands never dreamed of; part of the strange newness of the problem is that it cannot be understood in terms of the age-old material problems of man: poverty, sickness, hunger, cold. The women who suffer this problem have a hunger that food cannot fill. It persists in women whose husbands are struggling interns and law clerks, or prosperous doctors and lawyers; in wives of workers and executives who make $5,000 a year or $50,000. It is not caused by lack of material advantages; it may not even be felt by women preoccupied with desperate problems of hunger, poverty, or illness. And women who think it will be solved by more money, a bigger house, a second car, moving to a better suburb, often discover it gets worse.

It is no longer possible today to blame the problem on loss of femininity: to say that education and independence and equality with men have made American women unfeminine. I think, in fact, that this is the first clue to the mystery: the problem cannot be understood in the generally accepted terms by which scientists have studied women, doctors have treated them, counsellors have advised them, and writers have written about them. Women who suffer this problem have lived their whole lives in the pursuit of feminine fulfilment. They are not career women (although career women may have other problems); they are women whose greatest ambition has been marriage and children. For the oldest of these women, these daughters of the American middle class, no other dream was possible. The ones in their forties and fifties who once had other dreams gave them up and threw themselves joyously into life as housewives. For the youngest, the new wives and mothers, this was the only dream. They are the ones who quit high school and college to marry, or marked time in some job in which they had no real interest until they married.

Are the women who finished college, the women who once had dreams beyond housewifery, the ones who suffer the most? According to the experts they are, but listen to these four women:

> My days are all busy, and dull, too. All I ever do is mess around. I get up at eight – I make breakfast, so I do the dishes, have lunch, do some more dishes and some laundry and cleaning in the afternoon. Then it's supper dishes and I get to sit down a few minutes before the children have to be sent to bed . . . That's all there is to my day. It's just like any other wife's day. Humdrum. The biggest time, I am chasing kids.

> Ye Gods, what do I do with my time? Well, I get up at six. I get my son dressed and then give him breakfast. After that I wash dishes and bathe and feed the baby. Then I get lunch and while the children nap, I sew or mend or iron and do all the other things I can't get done before noon. Then I cook supper for the family and my husband watches TV while I do the dishes. After I get the children to bed, I set my hair and then I go to bed.

> The problem is always being the children's mommy, or the minister's wife and never being myself.

> A film made of any typical morning in my house would look like an old Marx Brothers' comedy. I wash the dishes, rush the older children off to school, dash out in the yard to cultivate the chrysanthemums,

run back in to make a phone call about a committee meeting, help the youngest child build a blockhouse, spend fifteen minutes skimming the newspapers so I can be well-informed, then scamper down to the washing machines where my thrice-weekly laundry includes enough clothes to keep a primitive village going for an entire year. By noon I'm ready for a padded cell. Very little of what I've done has been really necessary or important. Outside pressures lash me through the day. Yet I look upon myself as one of the more relaxed housewives in the neighbourhood. Many of my friends are even more frantic. In the past sixty years we have come full circle and the American housewife is once again trapped in a squirrel cage. If the cage is now a modern plateglass-and-broadloom ranch house or a convenient modern apartment, the situation is no less painful than when her grandmother sat over an embroidery hoop in her gilt-and-plush parlour and muttered angrily about women's rights.

The first two women never went to college. They live in developments in Levittown, New Jersey, and Tacoma, Washington, and were interviewed by a team of sociologists studying working-men's wives.[2] The third, a minister's wife, wrote on the fifteenth reunion questionnaire of her college that she never had any career ambitions, but wishes now she had.[3] The fourth, who has a PhD in anthropology, is today a Nebraska housewife with three children.[4] Their words seem to indicate that housewives of all educational levels suffer the same feeling of desperation.

The fact is that no one today is muttering angrily about 'women's rights', even though more and more women have gone to college. In a recent study of all the classes that have graduated from Barnard College,[5] a significant minority of earlier graduates blamed their education for making them want 'rights', later classes blamed their education for giving them career dreams, but recent graduates blamed the college for making them feel it was not enough simply to be a housewife and mother; they did not want to feel guilty if they did not read books or take part in community activities. But if education is not the cause of the problem, the fact that education somehow festers in these women may be a clue.

If the secret of feminine fulfilment is having children, never have so many women, with the freedom to choose, had so many children, in so few years, so willingly. If the answer is love, never have women searched for love with such determination. And yet there is a growing suspicion that the problem may not be sexual, though it must somehow be related to sex. I have heard from many doctors evidence of new sexual problems between man and wife – sexual hunger in wives so great their husbands cannot satisfy it. 'We have made woman a sex creature,' said a psychiatrist at the Margaret Sanger marriage counselling clinic. 'She has no identity except as a wife and mother. She does not know who she is herself. She waits all day for her husband to come home at night to make her feel alive. And now it is the husband who is not interested. It is terrible for the woman, to lie there, night after night, waiting for her husband to make her feel alive.' Why is there such a market for books and articles offering sexual advice? The kind of sexual orgasm which Kinsey found in statistical plenitude in the recent generations of American women does not seem to make this problem go away.

On the contrary, new neuroses are being seen among women – and problems as yet unnamed as neuroses – which Freud and his followers did not predict, with physical symptoms, anxieties, and defence mechanisms equal to those caused by sexual repression. And strange new problems are being reported in the growing generations of children whose mothers were always there, driving them around, helping them with their homework – an inability to endure pain or discipline or pursue any self-sustained goal of any sort, a devastating boredom with life. Educators are increasingly uneasy about the dependence, the lack of self-reliance, of the boys and girls who are entering college today. 'We fight a continual battle to make our students assume manhood,' said a Columbia dean.

A White House conference was held on the physical and muscular deterioration of American children: were they being overnurtured? Sociologists noted the astounding organization of suburban children's lives: the lessons, parties, entertainments, play and study groups organized for them. A suburban housewife in Portland, Oregon, wondered why the children 'need' Brownies and Boy Scouts out here.

> This is not the slums. The kids out here have the great outdoors. I think people are so bored, they organize the children, and then try to hook everyone else on it. And the poor kids have no time left just to lie on their beds and daydream.

When a woman tries to put the problem into words, she often merely describes the daily life she leads. What is there in this recital of comfortable domestic detail that could possibly cause such a feeling of desperation? Is she trapped simply by the enormous demands of her role as modern housewife: wife, mistress, mother, nurse, consumer, cook, chauffeur; expert on interior decoration, child care, appliance repair, furniture refinishing, nutrition, and education? Her day is fragmented; she can never spend more than fifteen minutes on any one thing; she has no time to read books, only magazines; even if she had time, she has lost the power to concentrate. At the end of the day, she is so terribly tired that sometimes her husband has to take over and put the children to bed.

This terrible tiredness took so many women to doctors in the 1950s that one decided to investigate it. He found, surprisingly, that his patients suffering from 'housewife's fatigue' slept more than an adult needed to sleep – as much as ten hours a day – and that the actual energy they expended on housework did not tax their capacity. The real problem must be something else, he decided – perhaps boredom. Some doctors told their women patients they must get out of the house for a day, treat themselves to a movie in town. Others prescribed tranquillizers. Many suburban housewives were taking tranquillizers like cough drops.

> You wake up in the morning, and you feel as if there's no point in going on another day like this. So you take a tranquillizer because it makes you not care so much that it's pointless.

It is easy to see the concrete details that trap the suburban housewife, the continual demands on her time. But the chains that bind her in her trap are chains made up of mistaken ideas and misinterpreted facts, of incomplete truths and unreal choices. They are not easily seen and not easily shaken off.

I found many clues by talking to suburban doctors, gynaecologists, obstetricians, child-guidance clinicians, pediatricians, high-school guidance counsellors, college professors, marriage counsellors, psychiatrists, and ministers – questioning them not on their theories, but on their actual experience in treating American women. I became aware of a growing body of evidence, much of which has not been reported publicly because it does not fit current modes of thought about women – evidence which throws into question the standards of feminine normality, feminine adjustment, feminine fulfilment, and feminine maturity by which most women are still trying to live.

I began to see in a strange new light the American return to early marriage and the large families that are causing the population explosion; the recent movement to natural child-birth and breastfeeding; suburban conformity, and the new neuroses, character pathologies and sexual problems being reported by the doctors. I began to see new dimensions to old problems that have long been taken for granted among women: menstrual difficulties, sexual frigidity, promiscuity, pregnancy fears, childbirth depression, the high incidence of emotional breakdown and suicide among women in their twenties and thirties, the menopause crises, the so-called passivity and immaturity of American men, the discrepancy between women's tested intellectual abilities in childhood and their adult achievement, the changing incidence of adult sexual orgasm in American women, and persistent problems in psychotherapy and in women's education.

If I am right, the problem that has no name stirring in the minds of so many American women today is not a matter of loss of femininity or too much education, or the demands of domesticity. It is far more important than anyone recognizes. It is the key to these other new and old problems which have been torturing women and their husbands and children, and puzzling their doctors and educators for years. It may well be the key to our future as a nation and a culture. We can no longer ignore that voice within women that says: 'I want something more than my husband and my children and my home.'

The Passionate Journey

It was the need for a new identity that started women, a century ago, on that passionate journey, that vilified, misinterpreted journey away from home.

It has been popular in recent years to laugh at feminism as one of history's dirty jokes: to pity, sniggering, those old-fashioned feminists who fought for women's rights to higher education, careers, the vote. They were neurotic victims of penis envy who wanted to be men, it is said now. In battling for women's freedom to participate in the major work and decisions of society as the equals of men, they denied their very nature as women, which fulfils itself only through sexual passivity, acceptance of male domination, and nurturing motherhood.

But if I am not mistaken, it is this first journey which holds the clue to much that has happened to women since. It is one of the strange blind spots of contemporary psychology not to recognize the reality of the passion that moved these women to leave home in search of a new identity, or, staying home, to yearn bitterly for something more. Theirs was an act of rebellion, a violent denial of the identity of women as it was then defined. It was the need for a new identity that led those passionate feminists to forge new trails for women. Some of those trails were unexpectedly rough, some were dead ends, and some may have been false, but the need for women to find new trails was real.

Changeless woman, childish woman, a woman's place is in the home, the feminists were told. But man was changing; his place was in the world and his world was widening. Woman was being left behind. Anatomy was her destiny; she might die giving birth to one baby, or live to be thirty-five, giving birth to twelve, while man controlled his destiny with that part of his anatomy which no other animal had: his mind.

Women also had minds. They also had the human need to grow. But the work that fed life and moved it forward was no longer done at home, and women were not trained to understand and work in the world. Confined to the home, a child among her children, passive, no part of her existence under her own control, a woman could only exist by pleasing man. She was wholly dependent on his protection in a world that she had no share in making: man's world. She could never grow up to ask the simple human question, 'Who am I? What do I want?'

Even if man loved her as a child, a doll, a decoration; even if he gave her rubies, satin, velvets; even if she was warm in her house, safe with her children, would she not yearn for something more? She was, at that time, so completely defined as object by man, never herself as subject, 'I', that she was not even expected to enjoy or participate in the act of sex. 'He took his pleasure with her . . . he had his way with her,' as the sayings went. Is it so hard to understand that emancipation, the right to full humanity, was important enough to generations of women, still alive or only recently dead, that some fought with their fists, and went to jail and even died for it? And for the right to human growth, some women denied their own sex, the desire to love and be loved by a man, and to bear children.

It is a strangely unquestioned perversion of history that the passion and fire of the feminist movement came from man-hating, embittered, sex-starved spinsters, from castrating, unsexed non-women who burned with such envy for the male organ that they wanted to take it away from all men, or destroy them, demanding rights only because they lacked the power to love as women. Mary Wollstonecraft, Angelina Grimké, Ernestine Rose, Margaret Fuller, Elizabeth Cady Stanton, Julia Ward Howe, Margaret Sanger all loved, were loved, and married; many seem to have been as passionate in their relations with lover and husband, in an age when passion in woman was as forbidden as intelligence, as they were in their battle for woman's chance to grow to full human stature. But if they, and those like Susan Anthony, whom fortune or bitter experience turned away from marriage, fought for a chance for woman to fulfil herself, not in relation to man, but as an individual, it was from a need as real and burning as the need for love. ('What woman needs,' said Margaret Fuller, 'is not as a woman to act or rule, but as a nature to grow, as an intellect to discern, as a soul to live freely, and unimpeded to unfold such powers as were given her.')

The feminists had only one model, one image, one vision,

of a full and free human being: man. For until very recently, only men (though not all men) had the freedom and the education necessary to realize their full abilities, to pioneer and create and discover, and map new trails for future generations. Only men had the vote: the freedom to shape the major decisions of society. Only men had the freedom to love, and enjoy love, and decide for themselves in the eyes of their God the problems of right and wrong. Did women want these freedoms because they wanted to be men? Or did they want them because they also were human?

That this is what feminism was all about was seen symbolically by Henrik Ibsen. When he said in the play *A Doll's House*, in 1879, that a woman was simply a human being, he struck a new note in literature. Thousands of women in middle-class Europe and America, in that Victorian time, saw themselves in Nora. And in 1960, almost a century later, millions of American housewives, who watched the play on television, also saw themselves as they heard Nora say:

> You have always been so kind to me. But our home has been nothing but a playroom. I have been your doll wife, just as at home I was Papa's doll child; and here the children have been my dolls. I thought it great fun when you played with me, just as they thought it fun when I played with them. That is what our marriage has been, Torvald . . .
>
> How am I fitted to bring up the children? . . . There is another task I must undertake first. I must try and

educate myself – you are not the man to help me in that. I must do that for myself. And that is why I am going to leave you now . . . I must stand quite alone if I am to understand myself and everything about me. It is for that reason that I cannot remain with you any longer . . .

Her shocked husband reminds Nora that woman's 'most sacred duties' are her duties to her husband and children. 'Before all else, you are a wife and mother,' he says. And Nora answers:

I believe that before all else I am a reasonable human being, just as you are – or, at all events, that I must try and become one. I know quite well, Torvald, that most people would think you right, and that views of that kind are to be found in books; but I can no longer content myself with what most people say or with what is found in books. I must think over things for myself and get to understand them . . .

Not very many women then, or even now, dared to leave the only security they knew – dared to turn their backs on their homes and husbands to begin Nora's search. But a great many, then as now, must have found their existence as housewives so empty that they could no longer savour the love of husband and children.

Some of them – and even a few men who realized that half the human race was denied the right to become fully human – set out to change the conditions that held women in bondage. Those conditions were summed up by the first Woman's Rights Convention in Seneca Falls, New York, in 1848, as woman's grievances against man:

> He has compelled her to submit to laws in the for-
> mation of which she has no voice . . . He has made
> her, if married, in the eyes of the law, civilly dead.
> He has taken from her all right to property, even to
> the wages she earns . . . In the covenant of mar-
> riage, she is compelled to promise obedience to her
> husband, he becoming to all intents and purposes
> her master – the law giving him power to deprive
> her of her liberty, and to administer chastisement . . .
> He closes against her all the avenues of wealth and
> distinction which he considers most honourable to
> himself. As a teacher of theology, medicine or law,
> she is not known. He has denied her the facilities for
> obtaining a thorough education, all colleges being
> closed against her . . . He has created a false public
> sentiment by giving to the world a different code of
> morals for men and women by which moral delin-
> quencies which exclude women from society are not
> only tolerated, but deemed of little account to man.
> He has usurped the prerogative of Jehovah himself,
> claiming it as his right to assign for her a sphere of
> action, when that belongs to her conscience and to
> her God. He has endeavoured in every way that he

could to destroy her confidence in her own powers,
to lessen her self-respect, and to make her willing to
lead a dependent and abject life.

It is hardly a coincidence that the struggle to free woman
began in America on the heels of the Revolutionary War, and
grew strong with the movement to free the slaves.[1] Thomas
Paine, the spokesman for the Revolution, was among the first
to condemn in 1775 the position of women 'even in countries
where they may be esteemed the most happy, constrained in
their desires in the disposal of their goods, robbed of freedom
and will by the laws, the slaves of opinion . . .' During the
Revolution, some ten years before Mary Wollstonecraft spear-
headed the feminist movement in England, an American
woman, Judith Sargent Murray, said woman needed knowledge to envision new goals and grow by reaching for them.
In 1837, the year Mount Holyoke opened its doors to give
women their first chance at education equal to men's, American women were also holding their first national anti-slavery
convention in New York. The women who formally launched
the women's rights movement at Seneca Falls met each other
when they were refused seats at an anti-slavery convention in
London. Shut off behind a curtain in the gallery, Elizabeth
Stanton, on her honeymoon, and Lucretia Mott, demure
mother of five, decided that it was not only the slaves who
needed to be liberated.

Whenever, wherever in the world there has been an up-
surge of human freedom, women have won a share of it for

themselves. Sex did not fight the French Revolution, free the
slaves in America, overthrow the Russian Tsar, drive the British
out of India; but when the idea of human freedom moves the
minds of men, it also moves the minds of women. The
cadences of the Seneca Falls Declaration came straight from
the Declaration of Independence:

> When, in the course of human events, it becomes
> necessary for one portion of the family of man to
> assume among the people of the earth a position
> different from that they have hitherto occupied . . .
> We hold these truths to be self-evident: that all men
> and women are created equal.

Feminism was not a dirty joke. The feminist revolution had
to be fought because women quite simply were stopped at a
stage of evolution far short of their human capacity. 'The
domestic function of woman does not exhaust her powers,'
the Rev. Theodore Parker preached in Boston in 1853. 'To make
one half the human race consume its energies in the functions
of housekeeper, wife and mother is a monstrous waste of the
most precious material God ever made.' And running like a
bright and sometimes dangerous thread through the history
of the feminist movement was also the idea that equality for
woman was necessary to free both man and woman for true
sexual fulfilment.[2] For the degradation of woman also
degraded marriage, love, all relations between man and
woman. After the sexual revolution, said Robert Dale Owen,
'then will the monopoly of sex perish with other unjust

monopolies; and women will not be restricted to one virtue, and one passion, and one occupation.'[3]

The women and men who started that revolution anticipated 'no small amount of misconception, misrepresentation, and ridicule'. And they got it. The first to speak out in public for women's rights in America – Fanny Wright, daughter of a Scotch nobleman, and Ernestine Rose, daughter of a rabbi – were called, respectively, 'red harlot of infidelity' and 'woman a thousand times below a prostitute'. The declaration at Seneca Falls brought such an outcry of 'Revolution', 'Insurrection Among Women', 'The Reign of Petticoats', 'Blasphemy', from newspapers and clergymen that the faint-hearted withdrew their signatures. Lurid reports of 'free love' and 'legalized adultery' competed with fantasies of court sessions, church sermons, and surgical operations interrupted while a lady lawyer or minister or doctor hastily presented her husband with a baby.

At every step of the way, the feminists had to fight the conception that they were violating the God-given nature of woman. Clergymen interrupted women's rights conventions, waving Bibles and quoting from the Scriptures: 'Saint Paul said: . . . and the head of every woman is man' . . . 'Let your women be silent in the churches, for it is not permitted unto them to speak' . . . 'And if they will learn anything, let them ask their husbands at home; for it is a shame for women to speak in the church' . . . 'But I suffer not a woman to teach, nor to usurp authority over the man, but to be in silence; for Adam was first formed, then Eve' . . . 'Saint Peter said: Likewise, ye wives, be in subjection to your own husbands' . . .

To give women equal rights would destroy that 'milder, gentler nature, which not only makes them shrink from, but disqualifies them for the turmoil and battle of public life,' a Senator from New Jersey intoned piously in 1866.

> They have a higher and a holier mission. It is in retiracy to make the character of coming men. Their mission is at home, by their blandishments, and their love, to assuage the passions of men as they come in from the battle of life, and not themselves by joining in the contest to add fuel to the very flames.

'They do not appear to be satisfied with having unsexed themselves, but they desire to unsex every female in the land,' said a New York assemblyman who opposed one of the first petitions for a married woman's right to property and earnings. Since 'God created man as the representative of the race', then 'took from his side the material for woman's creation' and returned her to his side in matrimony as 'one flesh, one being', the assembly smugly denied the petition: 'A higher power than that from which emanates legislative enactments has given forth the mandate that man and woman shall not be equal.'[4]

The myth that these women were 'unnatural monsters' was based on the belief that to destroy the God-given subservience of women would destroy the home and make slaves of men. Such myths arise in every kind of revolution that advances a new portion of the family of man to equality.

The name of Lucy Stone today brings to mind a man-eating fury, wearing pants, brandishing an umbrella. It took a long time for the man who loved her to persuade her to marry him, and though she loved him and kept his love throughout her long life, she never took his name. When she was born, her gentle mother cried: 'Oh, dear! I am sorry it is a girl. A woman's life is so hard.' A few hours before the baby came, this mother, on a farm in western Massachusetts in 1818, milked eight cows because a sudden thunderstorm had called all hands into the field: it was more important to save the hay crop than to safeguard a mother on the verge of childbirth. Though this gentle, tired mother carried the endless work of farmhouse and bore nine children, Lucy Stone grew up with the knowledge that 'There was only one will in our house, and that was my father's.'

She rebelled at being born a girl if that meant being as lowly as the Bible said, as her mother said. She rebelled when she raised her hand at church meetings and, time and again, it was not counted. At a church sewing circle, where she was making a shirt to help a young man through theological seminary, she heard Mary Lyon talk of education for women. She left the shirt unfinished, and at sixteen started teaching school for $1 a week, saving her earnings for nine years, until she had enough to go to college herself. She wanted to train herself 'to plead not only for the slave, but for suffering humanity everywhere. Especially do I mean to labour for the elevation of my own sex.' But at Oberlin, where she was one of the first women to graduate from the 'regular course', she had to practise public speaking secretly in the woods. Even at Oberlin, the girls were forbidden to speak in public.

> Washing the men's clothes, caring for their rooms, serving them at table, listening to their orations, but themselves remaining respectfully silent in public assemblages, the Oberlin 'co-eds' were being prepared for intelligent motherhood and a properly subservient wifehood.[5]

In appearance, Lucy Stone was a little woman, with a gentle, silvery voice which could quiet a violent mob. She lectured on abolition Saturdays and Sundays, as an agent for the Anti-Slavery Society, and for women's rights the rest of the week on her own – facing down and winning over men who threatened her with clubs, threw prayer books and eggs at her head, and once in mid-winter shoved a hose through a window and turned icy water on her.

In one town, the usual report was circulated that a big masculine woman, wearing boots, smoking a cigar, swearing like a trooper, had arrived to lecture. The ladies who came to hear this freak expressed their amazement to find Lucy Stone, small and dainty, dressed in a black satin gown with a white lace frill at the neck, 'a prototype of womanly grace . . . fresh and fair as the morning'.[6]

Her voice so rankled pro-slavery forces that the *Boston Post* published a rude poem promising 'fame's loud trumpet shall be blown' for the man who 'with a wedding kiss shuts up the mouth of Lucy Stone'. Lucy Stone felt that 'marriage is to a woman a state of slavery'. Even after Henry Blackwell had pursued her from Cincinnati to Massachusetts ('She was born locomotive,' he complained), and vowed to 'repudiate the supremacy of either woman or man in marriage', and wrote her: 'I met you at Niagara and sat at your feet by the whirlpool looking down into the dark waters with a passionate and unshared and unsatisfied yearning in my heart that you will never know, nor understand,' and made a public speech in favour of women's rights; even after she admitted that she loved him, and wrote, 'You can scarcely tell me any-thing I do not know about the emptiness of a single life,' she suffered blinding migraine headaches over the decision to marry him.

At their wedding, the minister Thomas Higginson reported that 'the heroic Lucy cried like any village bride'. The minister also said: 'I never perform the marriage ceremony without a renewed sense of the iniquity of a system by which man and wife are one, and that one is the husband.' And he sent to the newspapers, for other couples to copy, the pact which Lucy Stone and Henry Blackwell joined hands to make, before their wedding vows:

> While we acknowledge our mutual affection by publicly assuming the relationship of husband and wife . . . we deem it a duty to declare that this act on

our part implies no sanction of, nor promise of voluntary obedience to such of the present laws of marriage as refuse to recognize the wife as an independent, rational being, while they confer upon the husband an injurious and unnatural superiority.[7]

Lucy Stone, her friend, the pretty Reverend Antoinette Brown (who later married Henry's brother), Margaret Fuller, Angelina Grimké, Abbey Kelley Foster – all resisted early marriage, and did not, in fact, marry until in their battle against slavery and for women's rights they had begun to find an identity as women unknown to their mothers. Some, like Susan Anthony and Elizabeth Blackwell, never married; Lucy Stone kept her own name in more than symbolic fear that to become a wife was to die as a person. The concept known as *'femme couverte'* (covered woman), written into the law, suspended the 'very being or legal existence of a woman' upon marriage. 'To a married woman, her new self is her superior, her companion, her master.'

If it is true that the feminists were 'disappointed women', as their enemies said even then, it was because almost all women living under such conditions had reason to be disappointed. In one of the most moving speeches of her life, Lucy Stone said in 1855:

From the first years to which my memory stretches, I have been a disappointed woman. When, with my brothers, I reached forth after sources of knowledge, I was reproved with 'it isn't fit for you; it doesn't belong to women' . . . In education, in marriage, in religion, in everything, disappointment is the lot of woman. It shall be the business of my life to deepen this disappointment in every woman's heart until she bows down to it no longer.[8]

In her own lifetime, Lucy Stone saw the laws of almost every state radically changed in regard to women, high schools opened to them, and two thirds of the colleges in the United States. Her husband and her daughter, Alice Stone Blackwell, devoted their lives, after her death in 1893, to the unfinished battle for woman's vote. By the end of her passionate journey, she could say she was glad to have been born a woman. She wrote her daughter the day before her seventieth birthday:

I trust my Mother sees and knows how glad I am to have been born, and at a time when there was so much that needed help at which I could lend a hand. Dear Old Mother! She had a hard life, and was sorry she had another girl to share and bear the hard life of a woman . . . But I am wholly glad that I came.[9]

In certain men, at certain times in history, the passion for freedom has been as strong or stronger then the familiar passions of sexual love. That this was so, for many of those women who fought to free women, seems to be a fact, no matter how the strength of that other passion is explained. Despite the frowns and jeers of most of their husbands and fathers, despite the hostility if not outright abuse they got for their 'unwomanly' behaviour, the feminists continued their crusade. They themselves were tortured by soul-searching doubts every step of the way.

The call to that first Woman's Rights Convention came about because an educated woman, who had already participated in shaping society as an abolitionist, came face to face with the realities of a housewife's drudgery and isolation in a small town. Like the college graduate with six children in the suburb of today, Elizabeth Cady Stanton, moved by her husband to the small town of Seneca Falls, was restless in a life of baking, cooking, sewing, washing, and caring for each baby. Her husband, an abolitionist leader, was often away on business. She wrote:

> I now understood the practical difficulties most women had to contend with in the isolated household and the impossibility of woman's best development if in contact the chief part of her life with servants and children . . . The general discontent I felt with woman's portion . . . and the wearied, anxious look of the majority of women, impressed me with the strong feeling that some active measures should be taken . . . I could not see what to do or where to begin – my only thought was a public meeting for protest and discussion.[10]

She put only one notice in the newspapers, and housewives and daughters who had never known any other kind of life came in wagons from a radius of fifty miles to hear her speak.

However dissimilar their social or psychological roots, all who led the battle for women's rights, early and late, also shared more than common intelligence, fed by more than common education for their time. Otherwise, whatever their emotions, they would not have been able to see through the prejudices which had justified woman's degradation, and to put their dissenting voice into words. Mary Wollstonecraft educated herself and was then educated by that company of English philosophers then preaching the rights of man. Margaret Fuller was taught by her father to read the classics of six languages, and was caught up in the transcendentalist group around Emerson. Elizabeth Cady Stanton's father, a judge, got his daughter the best education then available, and supplemented it by letting her listen to his law cases. Ernestine Rose, the rabbi's daughter who rebelled against her religion's doctrine that decreed woman's inferiority to man, got her education in 'free thinking' from the great Utopian philosopher Robert Owen. She also defied orthodox religious custom to marry a man she loved. She always insisted, in the bitterest days of the fight for women's rights, that woman's enemy was not man. 'We do not fight with man himself, but only with bad principles.'

These women were not man-eaters. Julia Ward Howe, brilliant and beautiful daughter of the New York '400' who studied intensively every field that interested her, wrote the 'Battle Hymn of the Republic' anonymously, because her husband

believed her life should be devoted to him and their six children. She took no part in the suffrage movement until 1868,
when she met Lucy Stone, who

> . . . had long been the object of one of my imagin-
> ary dislikes. As I looked into her sweet, womanly
> face and heard her earnest voice, I felt that the object
> of my distaste had been a mere phantom, conjured
> up by silly and senseless misrepresentations . . .
> I could only say, 'I am with you.'[11]

The irony of that man-eating myth is that the so-called
excesses of the feminists arose from their helplessness. When
women are considered to have no rights nor to deserve any,
what can they do for themselves? At first, it seemed there was
nothing they could do but talk. They held women's rights
conventions every year after 1848, in small towns and large,
national and state conventions, over and over again – in Ohio,
Pennsylvania, Indiana, Massachusetts. They could talk till
doomsday about the rights they did not have. But how do
women get legislators to let them keep their own earnings,
or their own children after divorce, when they do not even
have a vote? How can they finance or organize a campaign to
get the vote when they have no money of their own, nor even
the right to own property?

The very sensitivity to opinion which such complete
dependence breeds in women made every step out of their
genteel prison a painful one. Even when they tried to change
conditions that were within their power to change, they met

ridicule. The fantastically uncomfortable dress 'ladies' wore then was a symbol of their bondage: stays so tightly laced they could hardly breathe, half a dozen skirts and petticoats, weighing ten to twelve pounds, so long they swept up refuse from the street. The spectre of the feminists taking the pants off men came partly from the 'Bloomer' dress – a tunic, knee-length skirt, ankle-length pantaloons. Elizabeth Stanton wore it, eagerly at first, to do her housework in comfort, as a young woman today might wear shorts or slacks. But when the feminists wore the Bloomer dress in public, as a symbol of their emancipation, the rude jokes, from newspaper editors, street-corner loafers, and small boys, were unbearable to their feminine sensitivities. 'We put the dress on for greater freedom, but what is physical freedom compared to mental bondage,' said Elizabeth Stanton and discarded her 'Bloomer' dress. Most, like Lucy Stone, stopped wearing it for a feminine reason: it was not very becoming, except to the extremely tiny, pretty Mrs Bloomer herself.

Still, that helpless gentility had to be overcome, in the minds of men, in the minds of other women, in their own minds. When they decided to petition for married women's rights to own property, half the time even the women slammed doors in their faces with the smug remark that they had husbands, they needed no laws to protect them. When Susan Anthony and her women captains collected 6,000 signatures in ten weeks, the New York State Assembly received them with roars of laughter. In mockery, the Assembly recommended that since ladies always get the 'choicest tidbits' at the table, the best seat in the carriage, and their choice of which side of the bed to lie on, 'if there is any inequity or oppression the gentlemen are the sufferers'. However, they would waive 'redress' except where both husband and wife had signed the petition. 'In such case, they would recommend the parties to apply for a law authorizing them to change dresses, that the husband may wear the petticoats and the wife the breeches.'

The wonder is that the feminists were able to win anything at all – that they were not embittered shrews but increasingly zestful women who knew they were making history. There is more spirit than bitterness in Elizabeth Stanton, having babies into her forties, writing Susan Anthony that this one truly will be her last, and the fun is just beginning – 'Courage, Susan, we will not reach our prime until we're fifty.' Painfully insecure and self-conscious about her looks – not because of treatment by men (she had suitors) but because of a beautiful older sister and mother who treated a crossed eye as a tragedy – Susan Anthony, of all the nineteenth-century feminist leaders, was the only one resembling the myth. She felt betrayed when the others started to marry and have babies. But despite the chip on her shoulder, she was no bitter spinster with a cat. Travelling alone from town to town, hammering up her meeting notices, using her abilities to the fullest as organizer and lobbyist and lecturer, she made her own way in a larger and larger world.

In their own lifetime, such women changed the feminine image that had justified woman's degradation. At a meeting while men jeered at trusting the vote to women so helpless that they had to be lifted over mud puddles and handed into carriages, a proud feminist named Sojourner Truth raised her black arm:

> Look at my arm! I have ploughed and planted and gathered into barns . . . and ain't I a woman? I could work as much and eat as much as a man – when I could get it – and bear the lash as well . . . I have borne thirteen children and seen most of 'em sold into slavery, and when I cried out with my mother's grief, none but Jesus helped me – and ain't I a woman?

That image of empty gentility was also undermined by the growing thousands of women who worked in the red-brick factories: the Lowell mill girls who fought the terrible working conditions which, partly as a result of women's supposed inferiority, were even worse for them than for men. But those women, who after a twelve- or thirteen-hour day in the factory still had household duties, could not take the lead in the passionate journey. Most of the leading feminists were women of the middle class, driven by a complex of motives to educate themselves and smash that empty image.

What drove them on? Lonely and racked with self-doubt, Elizabeth Blackwell, in that unheard-of, monstrous determination to be a woman doctor, ignored sniggers – and tentative passes – to do her anatomical dissections. She battled for the right to witness the dissection of the reproductive organs, but decided against walking in the commencement procession because it would be unladylike. Shunned even by her fellow physicians, she wrote:

> I am woman as well as physician . . . I understand now why this life has never been lived before. It is hard, with no support but a high purpose, to live against every species of social opposition . . . I should like a little fun now and then. Life is altogether too sober.[12]

In the course of a century of struggle, reality gave the lie to the myth that woman would use her rights for vengeful domination of man. As they won the right to equal education, the right to speak out in public and own property, and the right to work at job or profession and control their own earnings, the feminists felt less reason to be bitter against man. But there was one more battle to be fought. As M. Carey Thomas, the brilliant first president of Bryn Mawr, said in 1908:

> Women are one half the world, but until a century ago . . . women lived a twilight life, a half life apart, and looked out and saw men as shadows walking. It was a man's world. The laws were men's laws, the government a man's government, the country a man's country. Now women have won the right to higher education and economic independence. The right to become citizens of the state is the next and inevitable consequence of education and work

outside the home. We have gone so far; we must go farther. We cannot go back.[13]

The trouble was, the women's rights movement had become almost too respectable; yet without the right to vote, women could not get any political party to take them seriously. When Elizabeth Stanton's daughter, Harriet Blatch, came home in 1907, the widow of an Englishman, she found the movement in which her mother had raised her in a sterile rut of tea and cookies. She had seen the tactics women used in England to dramatize the issue in a similar stalemate: heckling speakers at public meetings, deliberate provocation of the police, hunger strikes in jail – the kind of dramatic non-violent resistance Gandhi used in India, or that the Freedom Riders now use in the United States when legal tactics leave segregation intact. The American feminists never had to resort to the extremes of their longer-sinned-against English counterparts. But they did dramatize the vote issue until they aroused an opposition far more powerful than the sexual one.

As the battle to free women was fired by the battle to free the slaves in the nineteenth century, it was fired in the twentieth by the battles of social reform, of Jane Addams and Hull House, the rise of the union movement, and the great strikes against intolerable working conditions in the factories. For the Triangle Shirtwaist girls, working for as little as $6 a week, as late as 10 o'clock at night, fined for talking, laughing, or singing, equality was a question of more than education or the vote. They held out on picket lines through bitter cold and hungry months; dozens were clubbed by police and dragged off in Black Marias. The new feminists raised money for the strikers' bail and food, as their mothers had helped the Underground Railroad.

The final battle for the vote was fought in the twentieth century by the growing numbers of college-trained women, led by Carrie Chapman Catt, daughter of the Iowa prairie, educated at Iowa State, a teacher and a newspaperwoman, whose husband, a successful engineer, firmly supported her battles. One group that later called itself the Woman's Party made continual headlines with picket lines around the White House. After the outbreak of the First World War, there was much hysteria about women who chained themselves to the White House fence. Maltreated by police and courts, they went on hunger strikes in jail and were finally martyred by forced feeding. Many of these women were Quakers and pacifists; but the majority of the feminists supported the war even as they continued their campaign for women's rights.

In this final battle, American women over a period of fifty years conducted 56 campaigns of referenda to male voters; 480 campaigns to get legislatures to submit suffrage amendments to voters; 277 campaigns to get state party conventions to include woman's suffrage planks; 30 campaigns to get presidential party conventions to adopt woman's suffrage plans, and 19 campaigns with 19 successive Congresses.[14] Someone had to organize all those parades, speeches, petitions, meetings, lobbying of legislators and Congressmen. The new feminists were no longer a handful of devoted women;

thousands, millions of American women with husbands, children, and homes gave as much time as they could spare to the cause. The unpleasant image of the feminists today resembles less the feminists themselves than the image fostered by the interests who so bitterly opposed the vote for women in state after state, lobbying, threatening legislators with business or political ruin, buying votes, even stealing them, until, and even after, thirty-six states had ratified the amendment.

The ones who fought that battle won more than empty paper rights. They cast off the shadow of contempt and self-contempt that had degraded women for centuries. The joy, the sense of excitement and the personal rewards of that battle are described beautifully by Ida Alexa Ross Wylie, an English feminist:

> To my astonishment, I found that women, in spite of knock-knees and the fact that for centuries a respectable woman's leg had not even been mentionable, could at a pinch outrun the average London bobby. Their aim with a little practice became good enough to land ripe vegetables in ministerial eyes, their wits sharp enough to keep Scotland Yard running around in circles and looking very silly. Their capacity for impromptu organization, for secrecy and loyalty, their iconoclastic disregard for class and established order were a revelation to all concerned, but especially themselves . . .

The day that, with a straight left to the jaw, I sent a fair-sized CID officer into the orchestra pit of the theatre where we were holding one of our belligerent meetings, was the day of my own coming of age . . . Since I was no genius, the episode could not make me one, but it set me free to be whatever I was to the top of my bent . . .

For two years of wild and sometimes dangerous adventure, I worked and fought alongside vigorous, happy, well-adjusted women who laughed instead of tittering, who walked freely instead of teetering, who could outfast Gandhi and come out with a grin and a jest. I slept on hard floors between elderly duchesses, stout cooks, and young shopgirls. We were often tired, hurt and frightened. But we were content as we had never been. We shared a joy of life that we had never known. Most of my fellow-fighters were wives and mothers. And strange things happened to their domestic life. Husbands came home at night with a new eagerness . . . As for children, their attitude changed rapidly from one of affectionate toleration for poor, darling mother to one of wide-eyed wonder. Released from the smother of mother love, for she was too busy to be more than casually concerned with them, they discovered that they liked her. She was a great sport. She had guts . . . Those women who stood outside the fight – I regret to say the vast majority – and who

> were being more than usually Little Women hated
> the fighters with the venomous rage of envy . . .[15]

Did women really go home again as a reaction to feminism?
The fact is that to women born after 1920, feminism was dead
history. It ended as a vital movement in America with the winning of that final right: the vote. In the 1930s and 1940s, the sort
of woman who fought for woman's rights was still concerned
with human rights and freedom – for Negroes, for oppressed
workers, for victims of Franco's Spain and Hitler's Germany.
But no one was much concerned with rights for women: they
had all been won. And yet the man-eating myth prevailed. The
feminists had destroyed the old image of woman, but they
could not erase the hostility, the prejudice, the discrimination
that still remained. Nor could they paint the new image of what
women might become when they grew up under conditions
that no longer made them inferior to men, dependent, passive,
incapable of thought or decision.

Most of the girls who grew up during the years when the
feminists were eliminating the causes of that denigrating 'genteel nothingness' got their image of woman from mothers
still trapped in it. These mothers were probably the real model
for the man-eating myth. The shadow of the contempt and
self-contempt which could turn a gentle housewife into a dom-
ineering shrew also turned some of their daughters into
angry copies of man. The first women in business and the
professions were thought to be freaks. Insecure in their new
freedom, some perhaps feared to be soft or gentle, love, have

children, lest they lose their prized independence, lest they be trapped again as their mothers were. They reinforced the myth.

But the daughters who grew up with the rights the feminists had won could not go back to that old image of genteel nothingness, nor did they have their aunts' or mothers' reasons to be angry copies of man, or fear to love them. They had come unknowing to the turning-point in woman's identity. They had truly outgrown the old image; they were finally free to be what they chose to be. But what choice were they offered? In that corner, the fiery, man-eating feminist, the career woman – loveless, alone. In this corner, the gentle wife and mother – loved and protected by her husband, surrounded by her adoring children. Though many daughters continued on the passionate journey their grandmothers had begun, thousands of others fell out – victims of a mistaken choice.

The real joke that history played on American women is not the one that makes people snigger, with cheap Freudian sophistication, at the dead feminists. It is the joke that Freudian thought played on living women, twisting the memory of the feminists into the man-eating phantom of the feminine mystique, shrivelling the very wish to be more than just a wife and mother. Encouraged by the mystique to evade their identity crisis, permitted to escape identity altogether in the name of sexual fulfilment, women once again are living in the old image of glorified femininity. And it is the same old image, despite its shiny new clothes, that trapped women for centuries and made the feminists rebel.

Notes

The Problem that Has No Name

1. See the Seventy-fifth Anniversary Issue of *Good Housekeeping*, May 1960, 'The Gift of Self', a symposium by Margaret Mead, Jessamyn West, *et al.*

2. Lee Rainwater, Richard P. Coleman, and Gerald Handel, *Working-man's Wife*, New York, 1959.

3. Betty Friedan, 'If One Generation Can Ever Tell Another', *Smith Alumnae Quarterly*, Northampton, Mass., Winter 1961. I first became aware of 'the problem that has no name' and its possible relationship to what I finally called 'the feminine mystique' in 1957, when I prepared an intensive questionnaire and conducted a survey of my own Smith College classmates fifteen years after graduation. This questionnaire was later used by alumnae classes of Radcliffe and other women's colleges with similar results.

4. Jhan and June Robbins, 'Why Young Mothers Feel Trapped', *Redbook*, September 1960.

5. Marian Freda Poverman, 'Alumnae on Parade', *Barnard Alumnae Magazine*, July 1957.

The Passionate Journey

1. See Eleanor Flexner, *Century of Struggle: The Woman's Rights Movement in The United States*, Cambridge, Mass., 1959. This definitive history of the woman's rights movement in the United States, published in 1959 at the height of the era of the feminine mystique, did not receive the attention it deserves, from either the intelligent

reader or the scholar. In my opinion, it should be required reading for every girl admitted to a US college. One reason the mystique prevails is that very few women under the age of forty know the facts of the woman's rights movement. I am much indebted to Miss Flexner for many factual clues I might otherwise have missed in my attempt to get at the truth behind the feminine mystique and its monstrous image of the feminists.

2. See Sidney Ditzion, *Marriage, Morals and Sex in America – A History of Ideas*, New York, 1953. This extensive bibliographical essay by the librarian of New York University documents the continuous inter-relationship between movements for social and sexual reform in America, and, specifically, between man's movement for greater self-realization and sexual fulfilment and the woman's rights movement. The speeches and tracts assembled reveal that the movement to emancipate women was often seen by the men as well as the women who led it in terms of 'creating an equitable balance of power between the sexes' for 'a more satisfying expression of sexuality for both sexes'.

3. ibid., p. 107.

4. Yuri Suhl, *Ernestine L. Rose and the Battle for Human Rights*, New York, 1959, p. 158. A vivid account of the battle for a married woman's right to her own property and earnings.

5. Flexner, op. cit., p. 30.

6. Elinor Rice Hays, *Morning Star, A Biography of Lucy Stone*, New York, 1961, p. 83.

7. Flexner, op. cit., p. 64.

8. Hays, op. cit., p. 136.

9. ibid., p. 285.

10. ibid., p. 73.

11. ibid., p. 221.

12. Flexner, op. cit., p. 117.

13. ibid., p. 235.

14. ibid., p. 173.

15. Ida Alexis Ross Wylie, 'The Little Woman', *Harper's*, November 1945.

1. MARTIN LUTHER KING, JR. · *Letter from Birmingham Jail*

2. ALLEN GINSBERG · *Television Was a Baby Crawling Toward That Deathchamber*

3. DAPHNE DU MAURIER · *The Breakthrough*

4. DOROTHY PARKER · *The Custard Heart*

5. *Three Japanese Short Stories*

6. ANAÏS NIN · *The Veiled Woman*

7. GEORGE ORWELL · *Notes on Nationalism*

8. GERTRUDE STEIN · *Food*

9. STANISLAW LEM · *The Three Electroknights*

10. PATRICK KAVANAGH · *The Great Hunger*

11. DANILO KIŠ · *The Legend of the Sleepers*

12. RALPH ELLISON · *The Black Ball*

13. JEAN RHYS · *Till September Petronella*

14. FRANZ KAFKA · *Investigations of a Dog*

15. CLARICE LISPECTOR · *Daydream and Drunkenness of a Young Lady*

16. RYSZARD KAPUŚCIŃSKI · *An Advertisement for Toothpaste*

17. ALBERT CAMUS · *Create Dangerously*

18. JOHN STEINBECK · *The Vigilante*

19. FERNANDO PESSOA · *I Have More Souls Than One*

20. SHIRLEY JACKSON · *The Missing Girl*

21. *Four Russian Short Stories*

22. ITALO CALVINO · *The Distance of the Moon*

23. AUDRE LORDE · *The Master's Tools Will Never Dismantle the Master's House*

24. LEONORA CARRINGTON · *The Skeleton's Holiday*

25. WILLIAM S. BURROUGHS · *The Finger*

26. SAMUEL BECKETT · *The End*

27. KATHY ACKER · *New York City in 1979*

28. CHINUA ACHEBE · *Africa's Tarnished Name*

29. SUSAN SONTAG · *Notes on 'Camp'*

30. JOHN BERGER · *The Red Tenda of Bologna*

31. FRANÇOISE SAGAN · *The Gigolo*

32. CYPRIAN EKWENSI · *Glittering City*

33. JACK KEROUAC · *Piers of the Homeless Night*

34. HANS FALLADA · *Why Do You Wear a Cheap Watch?*

35. TRUMAN CAPOTE · *The Duke in His Domain*

36. SAUL BELLOW · *Leaving the Yellow House*

37. KATHERINE ANNE PORTER · *The Cracked Looking-Glass*

38. JAMES BALDWIN · *Dark Days*

39. GEORGES SIMENON · *Letter to My Mother*

40. WILLIAM CARLOS WILLIAMS · *Death the Barber*

41. BETTY FRIEDAN · *The Problem that Has No Name*

42. FEDERICO GARCÍA LORCA · *The Dialogue of Two Snails*

43. YUKO TSUSHIMA · *Of Dogs and Walls*

44. JAVIER MARÍAS · *Madame du Deffand and the Idiots*

45. CARSON MCCULLERS · *The Haunted Boy*

46. JORGE LUIS BORGES · *The Garden of Forking Paths*

47. ANDY WARHOL · *Fame*

48. PRIMO LEVI · *The Survivor*

49. VLADIMIR NABOKOV · *Lance*

50. WENDELL BERRY · *Why I Am Not Going to Buy a Computer*